Chernobyl
1986:

An explosion at a nuclear power station

VIC PARKER

363.17
TS2025

www.raintreepublishers.co.uk
Visit our website to find out more information about **Raintree** books.

To order:
 Phone 44 (0) 1865 888113
Send a fax to 44 (0) 1865 314091
Visit the Raintree bookshop at **www.raintreepublishers.co.uk**
to browse our catalogue and order online.

First published in Great Britain by Raintree, Halley Court, Jordan Hill, Oxford OX2 8EJ, part of Harcourt Education.

Raintree is a registered trademark of Harcourt Education Ltd.

Editorial: Andrew Farrow and Christine Mc Cafferty
Design: Victoria Bevan and AMR Design Ltd
Illustrations: David Woodroffe
Picture Research: Maria Joannou and
    Ginny Stroud-Lewis
Production: Chloe Bloom

Originated by Modern Age
Printed and bound in China by South
    China Printing Company

10 digit ISBN 1 406 20285 1
13 digit ISBN 978 1 4062 0285 4

10 09 08 07 06
10 9 8 7 6 5 4 3 2 1

British Library Cataloguing in Publication Data
Parker, Vic
Chernobyl, 1986. - (When disaster struck)
363.1'799'09477
A full catalogue record for this book is available from the British Library.

Acknowledgements
The publishers would like to thank the following for permission to reproduce photographs:

Corbis 4 (Sygma/KOSTIN IGOR), 11 (Yann Arthus-Bertrand), 15 (Reuters), 19 (Mykhailo Markiv/Reuters), 21 (SYGMA/KOSTIN IGOR), 22 (Igor Kostin), 27 (sYGMA/KOSTIN IGOR), 31, 32 (Peter Turnley), 34 (SYGMA/KOSTIN IGOR), 36 (Igor Kostin), 37 (Gleb Garanich/Reuters), 38 (Bettmann), 41 (igor Kostin); Empics 17; Getty Images 40, 43 (AFP), 45 (AFP), 46 (AFP), 49 (AFP); John Frost Newspapers 30; Rex Features 16-17; RIA-Novosti 12, 14, 20, 23, 26, 28, 33; Topfoto 24, 29, 42.

Cover photograph of the wrecked Reactor Four at the Chernobyl nuclear power station, reproduced with permission of Rex Features.

The publishers would like to thank Cecelia Calhoun of The Children of Chernobyl US Alliance, Michael Mariotte of the Nuclear Information Resource Service, and David Lochbaum of the Union of Concerned Scientists for their assistance in the preparation of this book.

Every effort has been made to contact copyright holders of any material reproduced in this book. Any omissions will be rectified in subsequent printings if notice is given to the publishers.

The paper used to print this book comes from sustainable resources.

CONTENTS

Any words appearing in the text in bold, **like this**, are explained in the glossary.

AN EXPLOSION AT A NUCLEAR POWER STATION

Chernobyl, 1986

CHERNOBYL EXPLODES

Imagine you are a worker in an enormous nuclear power station. It is the middle of the night.

You are busy in a control room, manning rows of screens, gauges, switches, dials, and levers. Tonight a test is being run on the station.

The atmosphere is tense. Controlling a **nuclear reactor** is a complicated task. Suddenly a mighty BOOM shakes the building. Alarm sirens blare. The controls no longer work. Panic breaks out.

You run to the main hall. To your horror you find that the very **core** of the nuclear reactor has exploded. Nuclear fuel is on fire and is releasing invisible **radioactive particles** that can make humans extremely sick, or even cause a painful death.

This is what happened at the Chernobyl nuclear power station on 26 April 1986.

Checking the level of radioactive particles in the air near Chernobyl's exploded reactor four.

A DISASTER WAITING TO HAPPEN

Chernobyl, 1986

ESTONIAN S.S.R.
LATVIAN S.S.R.
LITHUANIAN S.S.R.

POLAND

EAST GERMANY

CZECHOSLOVAKIA

BYELORUSSIAN S.S.R.

Minsk

Kiev

Chernobyl

UKRAINIAN S.S.R.

EUROPE

HUNGARY

ROMANIA

YUGOSLAVIA

BULGARIA

ALBANIA

MOLDAVIAN S.S.R.

GEORGIAN S.S.R.

ARMENIAN S.S.R.

AZERBAIJAN S.S.R.

U.S.S.R.

RUSSIAN S.F.S.R.

KAZAKH S.S.R

KIRGIZ S.S.R.

TAJIK S.S.R.

UZBEK S.S.R.

TURKMEN S.S.R.

ASIA

AFRICA

N

KEY

Countries considered part of the Soviet Bloc and closely aligned to the U.S.S.R. in 1986

Other Communist countries

WHY WAS CHERNOBYL BUILT?

The Chernobyl nuclear power station was in Ukraine, which in 1986 was part of the Union of Soviet Socialist Republics (the USSR).

This was known as the Soviet Union. The Soviet Union covered nearly 22.5 million square kilometres (9 million square miles) of land.

Its **government** had to build power stations to provide enough electricity to develop the massive country.

Most power stations burn coal or oil. However, the Soviet Union did not have enough coal and oil to produce all the **electricity** it needed. It could not afford to buy enough from other countries. There were often electricity shortages in the Soviet Union that affected **industry** and people's homes. The Soviet government decided that building **nuclear power** stations was the answer.

Around 293 million people lived in the Soviet Union.

WHAT IS NUCLEAR POWER?

From the end of World War II (1945) until 1989 there was tension and competition between the governments and armies of the Soviet Union and those of the Western World.

In the Western world people **voted** and were allowed to develop their own businesses. In the world of **communism**, governments tried to control all business. It did not allow people freedom. The Soviet government wanted control of more countries. Although there was not a full-scale war, there was a struggle for power between the two groups.

The Soviet Union wanted to develop **nuclear weapons**, to keep up with the United States and the United Kingdom, which also had nucler weapons. This is another reason why the Soviet government wanted to produce nuclear energy. A by-product of nuclear power stations is the metal plutonium. Plutonium is necessary to make nuclear weapons.

Nuclear power is not made using coal or oil as fuel. It uses a metal called uranium. Burning coal and oil sends harmful gases, such as carbon dioxide, into the air. Scientists believe these gases are warming up the Earth and causing long-term **climate change**. Nuclear power stations release fewer of these harmful gases into the air.

Uranium comes from mining the earth, just like coal and oil. The Soviet Union had large amounts of uranium on its own land. Uranium does not need to be burned to produce heat. This is because it contains a **radioactive material** called uranium-235.

Scientists can make uranium-235 into long rods of fuel. Many of these rods are placed next to each other. When this happens, the **atoms** that make up uranium-235 start to split. This causes more to split. This is a nuclear reaction. A nuclear reaction gives off heat.

Neutron hits nucleus of a uranium-235 atom

Nucleus splits

Energy

Three more neutrons released, which hit other nucleii

Every atom has a nucleus. In a nuclear reaction, the nucleus of uranium-235 is split, releasing energy. This energy is then converted into electricity.

Hundreds of uranium-235 fuel rods heat water inside a gigantic, sealed steel container called a reactor. The reactor works a bit like an enormous kettle, except the steam does not escape. It goes through pipes to **turbines**, which drive generators, which produce **electricity**. The steam is around 580°C (1076°F). That is about three times as hot as a kitchen oven. The reactor has to be extremely strong to hold in the heat and pressure of the reaction. The whole thing weighs several thousand tons.

Most nuclear power stations are enormous. Two turbines and two generators need a hall about the size of a sports stadium.

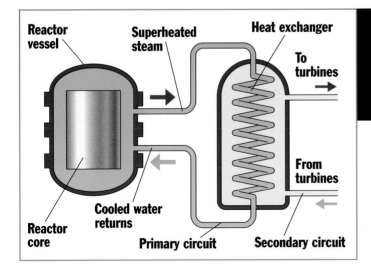

Reactor vessel

Superheated steam

Heat exchanger

To turbines

From turbines

Cooled water returns

Reactor core

Primary circuit

Secondary circuit

Nuclear energy is produced in a reactor core and channelled to a turbine.

THE DANGER OF NUCLEAR POWER

A nuclear reaction does not only release a huge amount of heat. It also releases tiny particles too small to see, called **radioactive particles**. When radioactive materials give off these particles, it is called radiation. Radiation can be very harmful to living things. If a person comes into contact with a high level, they can quickly become very ill with **radiation sickness**. The person may even die – within just two to four weeks.

If a person comes into contact with lower levels of radiation over many years, they may develop **cancer**. This can also cause them to die. Radiation can also make animals sick. It can poison the ground and make anything growing there **toxic**. It can cause plants to wither and die. It can poison water, killing fish. Radioactive particles can stay poisonous for thousands of years.

In a nuclear power station, the radioactive particles are meant to stay inside the reactor. However, nuclear reactions are much more difficult to control than the fires used to burn coal or oil in ordinary power stations. If a nuclear reactor gets out of control, it could cause an explosion or leak that might release dangerous radioactive material. For this reason workers at nuclear power stations have to be highly trained and follow strict safety rules. Most importantly nuclear reactors usually have emergency shutdown systems that work automatically if there is a problem.

The nuclear power station at Chernobyl was built from 1976 to 1979. We now know there were many safety problems at Chernobyl. The builders sometimes used the wrong measurements and poor quality materials.

GOVERNMENT SECRECY

The Soviet government sent inspectors to check how the Chernobyl power station was being built and operated. We now know that the inspectors reported to Moscow that there were safety problems. One report warned that the problems "could lead to mishaps and accidents". The Soviet government kept the reports secret and did nothing about them. There was a lot of secrecy around nuclear power because of its links to nuclear weapons. Also the Soviet Union wanted everyone to believe that their systems were better than those of the United States and the rest of the non-communist World.

The people in charge of operating the power station often rushed decisions and skipped **safety drills**. Many of the workers were poorly trained. Worst of all was the design of the four reactors that were built. Workers could turn off all the emergency shutdown systems. The reactors were also very unstable when they operated at low power.

Because of the secrecy around the USSR at this time, nuclear experts have had to try to guess exactly what happened on the night of the explosion, and in the days that followed.

A nuclear reactor is around 40 metres (125 feet) high. This is about as high as a 13-storey building. This reactor is in France.

DISASTER
STRIKES

Chernobyl, 1986

RUNNING TESTS

At 1:00 p.m. on Friday 25 April 1986, Anatoly Dyatlov was on duty at Chernobyl's reactor four.

Dyatlov was deputy chief **engineer**. He was getting ready to run some tests on the reactor. First, the reactor had to be slowed to its lowest operating power. To do this workers used a special crane to lower boron rods into the reactor. Boron is a metal that slows nuclear reactions. The boron rods slowed the reactor to half-power. Then the workers turned off one of the reactor's two turbines. All was going well.

At 2:00 p.m. the workers carried out the next stage for the tests. They turned off the emergency core-cooling system. This system would have automatically flooded the reactor with water, to cool the core, in case of a problem. Turning it off was against all safety rules.

This picture shows the Chernobyl power station before the explosion of 1986.

HEADING INTO DANGER

Soon after there was a phone call from an electricity official in Kiev. He was worried. If reactor four was slowed to lowest operating power, Kiev might run short of electricity. He asked Dyatlov to wait until night time, when most people in Kiev would be asleep. Then the city would not need so much electricity.

Dyatlov agreed to wait. He left the reactor running at half-power for nine hours – with the emergency core-cooling system turned off. At 11:10 p.m., late that night, he got the go-ahead from Kiev. Dyatlov at last ordered the reactor to be slowed to the lowest operating power.

In 1986 Kiev was the Soviet Union's third largest city. It had about 2.5 million residents at that time.

The control room was full of people. A representative from the equipment manufacturing company had come to watch the tests, as well as several important Chernobyl engineers. Two controllers, Alexander Akimov and Leonid Toptunov, must have been very nervous. They had the important job of checking that the reactor stayed under control as it slowed down.

Around midnight Akimov and Toptunov realized that the reactor had slipped to a level that was too low to do the test. It was heading for **shutdown**. The nuclear reaction was slowing to a stop.

Dyatlov insisted that they carry on with the test. He was angry. He ordered the workers to use the crane to lift out some boron cooling rods. This would speed up the reactor again. Akimov and Toptunov were worried that this was not safe. But they did as the deputy chief engineer told them. When the power had risen slightly, the water pumps were switched on. But switching on the pumps lowered the water level in other parts of the reactor. Like an empty kettle, the reactor began to boil dry.

Each of the four reactors had its own control room.

A SHOCKING ACCIDENT

Dyatlov now ordered his test to go ahead. At 1:23 a.m. they all heard some thumps that made the ground tremble under their feet.

Akimov and Toptunov watched the controls nervously. They saw a sudden huge **power surge**. Akimov pressed a button to lower all the cooling rods into the core, to slow the reaction down again. Suddenly the rods jammed. There was an enormous explosion and a blast shook the control room. Everyone was horrified. None of the reactor controls seemed to be working.

Panic broke out. Dyatlov and other engineers shouted orders. Some workers ran to finish lowering the cooling rods, by hand. Others went to try to turn the emergency core-cooling system on, also by hand. Both of these things were impossible to do, but the engineers still tried.

As the workers ran towards the reactor room, they found many corridors blown apart and in darkness. Enormous heat blasted them. One of the workers was **scalded** to death by steam.

Four desperate engineers ran up a staircase to see what had happened. They had to climb all the way to level 35. They stared down in horror at what they saw. The roof of the building was in tatters. Down below was a white-hot furnace. The core of reactor four was on fire. They rushed to report to the power station director at once. He could not believe what he was hearing.

We now know that reactor four raced out of control. It was making more heat than the cooling system could deal with and remove.

THE POWER OF THE EXPLOSION

The explosion sent 55 metric tonnes (60 US tons) of nuclear fuel into the atmosphere in the form of smoke and ash. At least 77 tonnes (85 US tons) of nuclear fuel and 220 tonnes (242 US tons) of radioactive graphite landed around the power plant. The reactor core, which was now on fire, contained a further 55 tonnes (60 US tons) of nuclear fuel and 880 tonnes (970 US tons) of graphite.

No emergency shutdown systems were on, so the heat caused vaporized water (steam) to build up. This caused a steam explosion. Air rushed in and set off another explosion in the core. Radioactive particles from the nuclear reaction were hurled high into the air. They created a cloud of invisible, but deadly radiation.

The extent of the damage could be seen from a helicopter. The explosion destroyed the concrete shield over the reactor.

FIGHTING THE FIRE

Three local fire engines were called to the power station. Some firefighters raced to put out small fires that had started all over the site. These had been caused by fiery material falling from the explosion. Other firefighters climbed up the outside of the reactor four building. They aimed their hoses at the raging volcano inside. They were horrified by the scale of the blaze. They called for more fire engines to come from the town of Pripyat and the city of Kiev. They needed as many as possible.

The firefighters could see there was a terrible danger. The enormous fire might spread to the other reactors. There were already fires on the roof of the reactor three building nearby. However, the dangers they could not see were far worse. The firefighters did not realize that this was not a normal fire. It could not be put out with water. Even worse, the burning reactor was giving off huge amounts of radiation. The firefighters were being exposed to the radiation.

The power station officials knew the dangers. However, they did not warn the firefighters. They did not warn local people either.

In total 186 firefighters and 81 fire engines arrived to tackle the fires at Chernobyl. They fought bravely and worked very hard through the night. The small fires were all put out by about 6:30 a.m. But the blaze still roared inside the core of reactor four. The firefighters were not making any difference to it.

Many of them were falling ill. Doctors soon realized they needed urgent treatment for radiation sickness.

"IT WAS COMING FROM US"

"They started measuring the radiation but it was too high. It was coming from us – dust, bits of graphite that were on us... I started to feel very tired. I felt sick. I wanted to lie down and have a rest – forget about everything. My body and face were glowing. People began to lose consciousness. They started vomiting and were taken to hospital."

Boris Aleshaev, one of the first firefighters on the scene. From *Children of Chernobyl*, Channel 4 TV

Radiation sickness first causes severe tiredness, vomiting, and diarrhoea. Sufferers may then get headaches, breathing pains and a bad cough. Their gums may bleed and their teeth and hair may fall out. Their skin may bruise and bleed.

Seriously ill firefighters, 129 in total, were flown to a special clinic in Moscow. Many of them had their bodies turn brown (a "nuclear tan"). Many fell into a fever and eventually, a **coma**. Most died. Doctors and nurses who care for people with radiation sickness have to be very careful that the radiation does not poison them too.

Relatives of firefighters march in Kiev in 2005 in memory of those who died. The firefighters bravely prevented the fire spreading to the other reactors.

LIFE AS USUAL

It was clear that a disaster had happened. But Chernobyl bosses did not shut down the other reactors. Hundreds of workers arrived to begin the day shift as usual. Many of them had been woken in the night by the blast. Now they were worried about the flames billowing out of reactor four. The bosses told the workers there had been a small explosion, but that there was nothing to worry about. They said everything was under control.

This is also what director Bryukhanov told the Soviet government on the telephone. However, the government sent experts on a jet to Chernobyl straight away to check. By midday the experts were in a helicopter, flying around the power station. They were horrified by what they saw. They knew that the fire could go on burning for weeks, or even months. They believed there was only one way to put it out. This was to bury the fire by dropping tons of sand, lead, clay, and boron on top of it. The experts hoped this might also absorb the radiation caused by the fire and prevent the damaged reactor from restarting.

The nearby Ukrainian town of Pripyat in 1986. The town was especially built to house the Chernobyl workers and their families.

The townspeople of Pripyat spent that Saturday as normal. They went shopping, sat in their gardens, and visited friends. The children went to school to practise for a May Day parade.

As the day wore on, some people grew nervous. They heard about firefighters and workers at Chernobyl falling ill and being taken to hospital. Doctors arrived at the schools to give **iodine** tablets to the children. But no one was told why. Iodine can protect human bodies against some types of harmful radiation.

Later, policemen told them to stay indoors with the windows closed. Again, no one was told why. It was to keep the radiation in the air out of their houses. That evening the people of Pripyat saw helicopters swooping around the reactor, dropping huge sacks. Still, no one told them why.

The fire was very intense, burning at around 2,500°C (4,500°F). That is about 13 times hotter than an oven. Helicopters dropped sand and other materials on it.

EVACUATION

The Moscow experts and Chernobyl officials were measuring radiation around the power station. Levels of radiation were extremely high and dangerous. Some helicopter pilots had radiation sickness. They were too weak and ill to fly. Other pilots replaced them.

During Saturday night the government ordered buses from Kiev to Pripyat. On Sunday morning an official made a loudspeaker announcement to the people of Pripyat. He said an accident at the power station had caused an "unfavourable radiation situation". He said everyone had to leave Pripyat for a few days.

The alarmed people hurried to pack a few belongings. That afternoon, about 50,000 residents were driven away on 1200 buses and 200 lorries. The **convoy** stretched for 32 kilometres (18.6 miles).

Evacuees were told to take only a few personal belongings and their identity papers with them.

They thought they were just going for a few days. Many were worried about leaving their pets. They did not know that they would never see their homes again.

They were **evacuated** to Kiev and other nearby towns and villages. Schools and community centres were set up as shelters. The local people wondered what was going on. Little did they know that dangerous radiation was spreading towards them on the wind.

Soldiers tested cars and other vehicles for radiation in the area around Chernobyl.

On Monday 28 April, more than 48 hours later, the Soviet government still had not made an official announcement about the accident. That morning workers at a science institute in Kiev noticed something strange. Their work often involved handling radioactive materials. So there was equipment at the institute that checked them for harmful radiation. That day, the equipment picked up radiation as people went *into* the building. It was coming off people who had used buses that had been in Pripyat.

Meanwhile, back at Chernobyl, an **exclusion zone** was set up around the power station. Guards patrolled 10 kilometres (6.2 miles) of land. They would not allow anyone to go in. Reactors one, two, and three were shut down. Helicopter pilots were still trying to bury the fire in reactor four. But radiation was still rising from it and being carried northwards by the wind.

DOSIMETER

Scientists use a dosimeter to measure radiation. When reactor four exploded, the radiation level at Chernobyl hit the top of the dosimeter scale. There was 15,000 times more radiation than usually affects a person over a whole year. Later, scientists estimated that the radiation released because of the explosion was the same as nearly 100 nuclear bombs.

EMERGENCY AROUND THE WORLD

WORLD

Chernobyl, 1986

THE RADIATION SPREADS

Sweden is over 1,500 kilometres (over 900 miles) north of Chernobyl.

On Monday 28 April 1986, an alarm went off at the Forsmark nuclear power station in Sweden. The alarm warned of unusually high levels of radiation. At first the Forsmark engineers thought their own power station was leaking radioactivity. However, reports of high radiation soon came from scientists all over Sweden, Finland, Denmark, and Norway.

Swedish experts studied the radiation levels in these places, and the wind speed and direction. They tracked down the source of the radiation to the Chernobyl power station. They contacted the Soviet government, who said there was no problem. But at 9:00 p.m. the Soviet news announced the accident. However, they did not give any details or mention radiation.

A satellite photograph helped pinpoint Chernobyl's reactor as the source of radiation being picked up in Sweden and the rest of Scandinavia.

THE THREAT IN EUROPE

THE EFFECTS OF RADIATION

Very high doses of radiation can cause the skin, bones, and internal organs to break down. Death usually occurs within weeks. Low-level exposure can affect a person's **DNA**. This can lead to birth defects such as sterility and brain damage. Low-level exposure can also cause bone-marrow damage. This results in people's bodies being less able to fight disease. Many develop cancers like leukaemia or thyroid, breast, and lung cancers.

By this time the radiation had already done much damage in and around Sweden. Heavy rain fell, carrying radiation with it. In the north is a region called Lapland. Much of the land is covered with a plant called lichen. Reindeer lived in the region, eating the lichen. The lichen soaked up the radiation like a sponge soaks up water.

Over 700,000 Lapp people herded the reindeer, following an ancient lifestyle. They used the reindeer for transport, meat, skins for clothing, and bones for tools. The reindeer were later found to be full of radiation from feeding on the radioactive lichen. If the Lapps ate meat from these animals, it could damage their health. Meat from 50,000 reindeer had to be destroyed. The Lapps were also told that the lichen might be poisonous for many years. Their whole way of life was under threat.

Many vehicles that travelled through affected areas were hosed down to stop the danger spreading.

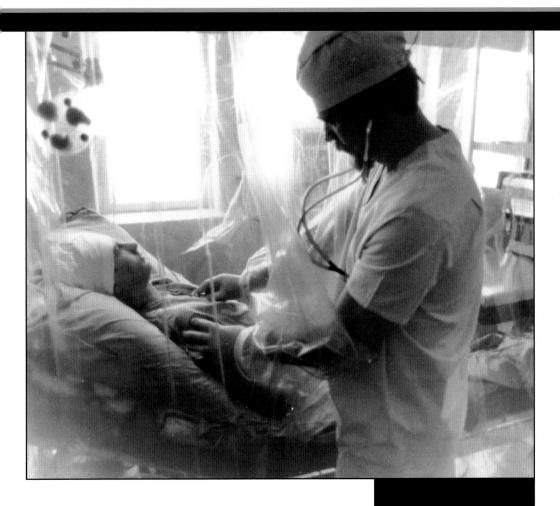

On Tuesday 29 April, the wind at Chernobyl changed direction. It carried the radiation to Poland, Germany, and Holland. In some places radiation levels were 500 times higher than normal. Some Polish farm workers became ill with radiation sickness.

The governments of these countries warned people to stay indoors. They told farmers to keep their animals inside. This was because the grass was poisoned by radiation, so it was not safe for grazing. The governments told people not to drink milk, in case the cows had been affected. They also told people not to eat fresh fish, meat, vegetables, or fruit.

Plastic tents were put up around patients to protect doctors and nurses from radioactive particles. Staff cared for the patients by reaching through long tubes in the tents' sides.

NO WARNING IN THE USSR

The Soviet government told its own people very little. It did not want to admit that there was a disaster. People there were cut off from the rest of the world. They did not know what was happening elsewhere.

Chernobyl was briefly mentioned in the television news in the Soviet Union on Tuesday 29 April. The report said that two people had died in the accident, but there were still no warnings about radiation. On 30 April it was said on the news that 197 people were in hospital with radiation sickness, but that the radiation levels were falling. It did not mention that the radiation levels were still dangerously high.

Thursday 1 May was Workers' Day (May Day). Street parades were held in cities and towns. In Kiev people flooded the streets. They had no idea that radiation from Chernobyl had reached them two days before. They were enjoying themselves in radiation that was 100 times higher than the official safe level.

Workers' Day was an important day in the communist Soviet Union.

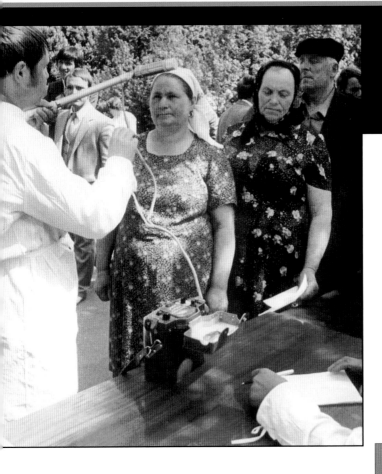

Evacuees from the Chernobyl area being checked for radiation at a state farm.

At Chernobyl, officials thought the fire was finally out. But radiation was still high. On 2 May the Soviet government ordered that the **exclusion zone** be made bigger. Around 130,000 people who lived within 30 kilometres (18.6 miles) of the power station were evacuated and taken to different centres.

On Saturday 3 May, radiation around Chernobyl started to rise again. The fire was not out! Burying it had made it hotter. Now it was burning down. If it burned too deep, radiation might get into underground water supplies to millions of people. Engineers risked their lives on a dangerous mission. They tunnelled under the reactor, emptied a big water tank there, and filled it with concrete. They hoped this would halt the spread of the radiation and the fire, too.

"I'LL NEVER GO BACK"

Chernobyl reactor four controller, Alexander Akimov, was treated in hospital for radiation sickness. During this time, he said:
"My chances are slim, but if I do survive, one thing is for sure: I'll never go back to work in the nuclear field. I'll do anything . . . I'll start my life from scratch, but I'll never go back to reactors."

From *Ablaze – The Story of Chernobyl* by Piers Paul Read

AROUND THE WORLD

Meanwhile the cloud of radiation travelled down to Greece, and across Austria, Italy, and France. Governments warned people not to drink rainwater. They ordered huge amounts of milk and fresh fruit and vegetables to be destroyed. The Austrian government told farmers not to let cows out to graze.

The radiation spread across Britain on 2 and 3 May, a week after the explosion. Most fell on hilly areas where sheep graze. The government ordered that flocks in these areas must not go into other areas. They could not be sold for meat.

People all over Europe became worried about the dangers. Some panicked. Some people in Germany drank liquid iodine. They hoped this would protect them from the radiation. They became ill and had to be rushed to hospital. People in Greece crowded into supermarkets to buy canned foods and bottled water. Police were brought in to control them.

Within days the disaster made headlines in the United States and around the world.

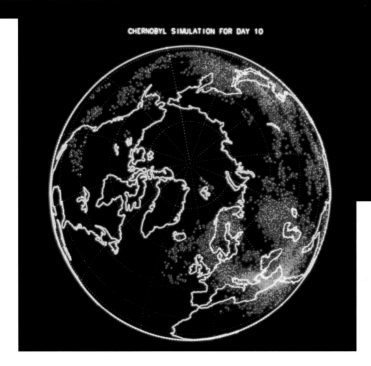

CHERNOBYL SIMULATION FOR DAY 10

This computer simulation shows how radioactive material from Chernobyl spread around the world in the first ten days. The areas affected within ten days are shown in pink.

By 5 May increased radiation levels were measured in western parts of the United States. The government assured people that it was within safe limits. Many experts disagreed. The United States government did checks at airports and seaports to measure radiation on travellers coming from Europe and the Soviet Union. This was also done in Canada and Japan.

Meanwhile the 2.5 million residents of Kiev had still not been told that radiation was high in their city. But now inspectors began checking for radiation in milk, meat, and vegetables in shops and on farms. They took poisoned food away to be destroyed. Rumours spread. Some people said that government officials knew radiation levels were high and were leaving Kiev. Others said drinking vodka and eating beetroot could protect against radiation. This is not true.

People panicked. From 5 May, ten days after the explosion, there was a rush to leave Kiev. Cars jammed the roads. People packed the bus and train stations. But no one knew where was safe to go.

THE END OF THE FIRE

At Chernobyl, on 6 May, the levels of radioactive particles coming from the reactor fire went down. By 9 May, the fire was just a glow. That day helicopter pilots dropped more tons of lead on top of it. On 10 May the fire was out at last. In total over 5,000 tons of sand, boron, lead, and other material had been dropped on it.

On that day reactor four controller, Alexander Akimov, died in the radiation sickness clinic in Moscow. His fellow controller, Leonid Toptunov, died four days later. Other Chernobyl workers and firefighters in the clinic were dying too. They were buried in a new cemetery outside Moscow, called Mitino. Their bodies were put in coffins lined with lead, to stop radiation seeping from them into the soil.

On 14 May Soviet President Mikhail Gorbachev at last talked to the world about the Chernobyl explosion. He appeared on television and admitted the huge scale of the disaster and its dangers.

Mikhail Gorbachev on Soviet TV. He promised that the radioactivity around the power station would be cleaned up.

Guards in protective clothing kept people out of Chernobyl's exclusion zone.

However, the effects of the disaster were far from over. By late May radiation in Kiev was still high. City officials sent children away to summer camps, because young people can be even more seriously affected by radiation than adults. The city's food came from surrounding farms, which were radioactive. There were no emergency stores of safe supplies.

In countries all over Europe, for months there were warnings not to go out in the rain or eat fresh foods. Governments sent gangs of workers to wash down buildings and streets. In many major cities, people went on marches to protest against nuclear power.

TIMELINE

26 April 1986 1:23 a.m. Chernobyl's reactor four explodes.

27 April 1986 2:00 p.m. The nearby town of Pripyat is evacuated.

28 April 1986 High levels of radiation are recorded in Scandinavia.

28 April 1986 9:00 p.m. Under pressure from foreign countries, the Soviet government admits that an accident has happened, but gives no details.

29 April 1986 Radiation reaches Poland, Germany, and Holland.

1 May 1986 The reactor fire seems to be out, but it is not. Radiation spreads across Greece, Austria, Italy, and France.

2 May 1986 A 30 kilometre (18.6 mile) zone around the power station is evacuated. Radiation reaches the United Kingdom.

5 May 1986 Radiation reaches western parts of the United States.

10 May 1986 The reactor fire is finally put out.

CLEANING UP AFTER THE DISASTER

Chernobyl, 1986

THE LIQUIDATORS

After the reactor four fire was out, the nuclear fuel in the reactor core was buried.

However it was still giving off dangerous radiation. Chunks of graphite, steel, and concrete from the explosion lay on the roof and all around.

The Soviet government brought robots from Germany to move all the rubble. The area was so radioactive that the robots could not work. There was no choice but to use people instead. Soldiers were ordered to do some of the work. The Soviet government offered big payments to other people to tempt them to help.

The workers were known as liquidators. About 800,000 people helped. Their work was very dangerous. Experts worked out that each person could only spend 90 seconds in the power station before the radiation harmed them.

Liquidators had to wear protective bodysuits and helmets. Their aprons were made of lead.

CLEANING UP THE LAND

There was a huge amount of work to be done around the power station. A vast area of forest had been scorched by the radiation. Thousands of animals and birds had been killed or left very ill.

The liquidators shot any sick or dying animals to put them out of their suffering. They also chopped down thousands of dead trees. The dead trees could not be burned because the ash and smoke would also have been radioactive. Instead the liquidators dug massive pits and lined them with concrete. Using bulldozers, they scooped up all the soil and trees and dropped them into the pits. Then they covered them with more concrete.

Thousands of contaminated vehicles used in the clean-up operations had to be buried in trenches. This is because metal absorbs radiation.

The liquidators also had to wash and scrub every inch of local towns and villages with special chemicals. Over 60,000 buildings were highly radioactive.

Nuclear experts designed a steel and concrete shell to put around the destroyed reactor. This was intended to trap radioactive particles that will continue to come from it for thousands of years.

Thousands of builders and miners risked their health to construct the shell. The shell was called the "sarcophagus", which means "stone coffin" in Latin. It took until the end of 1986 to build. By then, reactors one, two and three had been restarted.

"TERRIBLE PAIN"

"[Animals] crawled, half alive, along the road, in terrible pain. Birds looked as if they had crawled out of water, unable to fly or walk. [There were] cats with dirty fur, as if it had been burnt in places."

Nikolai Goshchitsky was a liquidator who worked in Pripyat in June 1986. From *The Legacy of Chernobyl* by Zhores A. Medvedev

LASTING
EFFECTS
OF THE
DISASTER

Chernobyl, 1986

INVESTIGATING THE CAUSE

The Soviet government often kept information from the Soviet people and the rest of the world.

However, the new President, Mikhail Gorbachev, wanted this to stop. Gorbachev ordered an enquiry into the causes of the Chernobyl disaster. He promised to tell the world what was found. He also wanted to work with other leaders to stop nuclear disasters happening elsewhere.

Soviet experts carried out the enquiry. They blamed the accident mostly on the people who worked at the station. In July 1987 several Chernobyl officials were put on trial. The experts did not admit that the unsafe design of the power station had partly caused the disaster. If they had, people all over the world would have demanded that all power stations built to the same design were closed. The Soviet Union could not afford this.

In October 1986, Gorbachev met with US President Ronald Reagan to discuss nuclear power and its dangers.

POLITICAL AND FINANCIAL COSTS

Five Chernobyl officials were found guilty of breaking safety rules, and were sentenced to prison. They included the power station director, Victor Bryukhanov, and the deputy chief engineer, Anatoli Dyatlov.

The Soviet government needed to keep Chernobyl running. If it was shut down, there would be power shortages for millions of people. A new town, Slavutich, was built for all the workers 30 kilometres (18.6 miles) away from the power station. The government said that, because of the clean-up, radiation levels were low enough to work in. But it set up checkpoints for kilometres around the power station to monitor the area and check people for radiation.

The people of Belarus protest in 1989 against the ongoing effects of Chernobyl .

During 1987, around 1,500 people whose homes had been in the exclusion zone moved back. However, most people from the area were too afraid of the radiation to return. Today there are so few people living in the former exclusion zone that it is like a ghost land.

This villager lives in an evacuated village. She has just walked 12 kilometres (7.5 miles) to buy bread. Apart from bread, she survives on food grown on a plot of land and mushrooms from the forest. The ground still has high radiation levels.

The Chernobyl disaster caused many Soviet people to lose trust in their government. The human suffering and high cost of the disaster weakened the USSR. For these and other reasons, the USSR broke up into separate countries in 1991. The land worst affected by radiation lies in Belarus, Ukraine, and Russia.

Their governments still have to pay for cleaning up large contaminated areas. Hundreds of thousands of people lived in these areas. The governments have had to build new homes for them elsewhere. These people lost their jobs, so the governments have had to pay them compensation and financial support.

Much of the contaminated land was farm land. Belarus cannot use 22 per cent of its farm land. The countries have had to spend money on trying to produce or buy enough safe food for their people. The governments have had to pay for treating people's health problems caused by the disaster too. All this is still being paid for today. It has cost hundreds of billions of pounds. It has also cost countries far away much money. Swedish officials estimated that the accident cost Sweden at least £82 million (US $144 million) in ruined agricultural products.

"A FIASCO"

"For thirty years, you scientists, specialists and ministers have been telling us that everything was safe [...] But now we have ended up with a fiasco.

"Chernobyl shed light on many of the sicknesses of our system [...] the concealing or hushing up of accidents and other bad news, irresponsibility and carelessness [...] The accident [...] was graphic evidence not only of how obsolete [out of date] our technology was, but also of the failure of the old system [communism]."

Mikhail Gorbachev's *Memoirs* (Doubleday, 1995)

HEALTH COSTS

Thirty-one people died due to the explosion. This is a matter of controversy, but it seems that thousands more have died or become ill because of the effects of the disaster. Many have suffered terrible stress. More than 200,000 people had to leave their homes.

There has never been a radiation leak on this scale before. Experts are not sure which illnesses the radiation might have caused, or for how long the radiation will cause illnesses in future. Reports differ widely. The governments of Belarus, Ukraine, and Russia say that about 25,000 liquidators have died so far from illnesses due to radiation. But the Liquidators' Committee says it is about 100,000.

In 2002, a United Nations report said that 8,000 people may develop **thyroid cancer**. However, World Health Organization projects have calculated this figure to be 50,000.

Medical specialists in countries affected by the disaster have reported a rise in other cancers and also a rise in babies born with abnormalities. Many people, especially children, suffer ill health today because of eating poor quality food produced on contaminated land.

Hospitals in Ukraine and Belarus were crowded with children affected by the radiation. The hospitals are still overburdened.

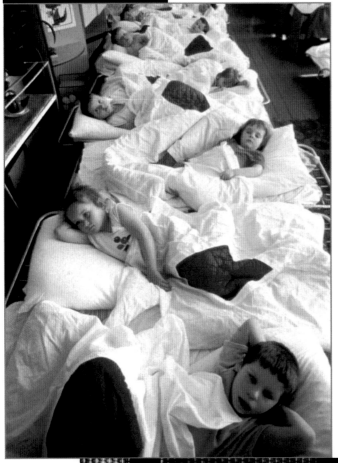

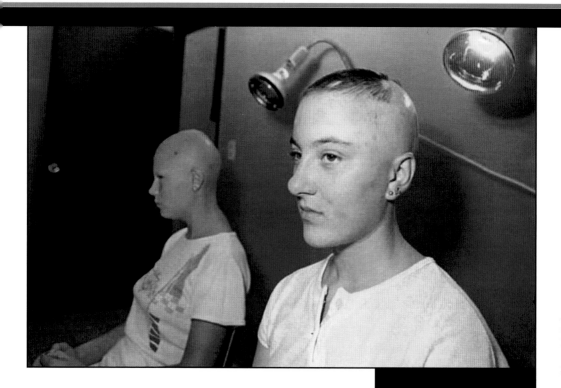

Immediately after the disaster, Western governments sent nuclear experts, doctors, and equipment to assist. Since then, they have sent millions of dollars in aid. They have also given money to make the badly designed Soviet nuclear reactors safer. Western governments also paid for thousands of Soviet engineers to visit Western nuclear power stations to see safety standards.

Two teenage girls get infra-red treatment at a children's hospital. This is part of a project to help people who have been exposed to dangerous radiation.

There are also many non-government organizations all over the world helping people cope with the effects of the disaster. Children of Chernobyl is an international project. It raises money for food, medicines, and medical equipment to be sent to affected areas. It also pays for children from contaminated areas to go to on holidays to other countries, such as the United States and the United Kingdom. Other charities are the Physicians of Chernobyl (Ukraine), Aid for Chernobyl Children (Germany), and the Canadian Relief Fund for Chernobyl Victims in Belarus (Canada).

CHERNOBYL IS SHUT DOWN

In 1991 the Chernobyl power station ran into problems once again. A fire broke out in a reactor two turbine hall. The Soviet government decided that it was too badly damaged to repair, so they shut down the reactor. The fire made it clear that the power station was not safe.

After negotiations with international organizations, the Ukrainian government agreed to shut down the power station. Reactor one was shut down at the end of 1996. On 15 December 2000, the final reactor (reactor three) was shut down and the power station closed for good. There was a special ceremony. Important guests from ten countries attended. It was broadcast on Ukrainian television. Afterwards, there was a church service in Kiev to remember those who had died in the disaster 14 years before.

By 1996 the concrete shell (sarcophagus) had begun crumbling. Holes appeared in the walls. They were so big that birds and animals were going in and out. Rainwater was running in, and leaking through the reactor building into the soil. People feared that the roof might collapse. There are still tons of radioactive fuel, waste, and dust inside, giving off radiation. The temperature inside is over 200°C (392 °F).

The Ukrainian government and international experts have had to repair the sarcophagus. They also plan to build a new, strengthened shell around it by 2009. The cost is nearly £460 million (US $810 million), paid by countries worldwide. The sarcophagus will need to be kept in good condition for thousands of years before the danger from radiation stops completely.

In 2000 Chernobyl's reactor three was switched off forever. The president of the Ukraine watched as an engineer turned it off. The event was broadcast live on television.

"STOP CHERNOBYL"

"To fulfil a state decision and Ukraine's international obligations, I hereby order the early stopping of the operation of reactor number three at the Chernobyl nuclear power plant."

Ukrainian President, Leonid Kuchma, at the closure of the Chernobyl power station.

The European Union has provided money and expert help to Ukraine to build two new reactors to replace the Chernobyl power station. These will be built with new safer designs. Some countries have urged Ukraine to use safer forms of power.

COULD IT HAPPEN AGAIN?

Chernobyl, 1986

FUTURE OF ENERGY SUPPLIES

Since the Chernobyl disaster, countries such as France, Russia, and Ukraine have built more nuclear power stations.

Other countries have stopped developing nuclear power stations altogether. These include Denmark, Australia, New Zealand, and the Philippines. In 2005, nuclear power was the second slowest-growing source of energy in the world.

Organizations such as Greenpeace believe there are safer, better alternatives to nuclear power stations and to power stations fired by coal and oil. These involve using energy from the sun's rays (solar energy), energy from the wind, and energy from moving water (**hydroelectricity**).

These forms of power are called "renewable energy". Many countries are developing and using them.

Today the town of Pripyat lies deserted. When people left, many things were left just as they were. Books and papers were even left on the school desks.

NUCLEAR POWER AROUND THE WORLD

Today there are 440 nuclear power station reactors in 31 countries. Nuclear power provides around 16 per cent of the world's energy. Some experts believe that modern nuclear power stations are perfectly safe. However, other experts are still worried, especially about storing the radioactive waste. Plutonium-239 will continue to be dangerous for 240,000 years.

Nuclear power stations produce only a small amount of waste. Much of it has low levels of radiation. This includes protective clothing, tools, and cleaning equipment. However, used fuel and reactor equipment are highly radioactive. All radioactive waste has to be stored away from living things for many thousands of years, until the radiation coming from it has faded away.

Some highly radioactive waste is stored in specially designed pools of water. The water cools the fuel and acts as a radiation barrier. The pools are kept safe inside strong, sealed buildings. Other highly radioactive waste is kept in containers made of thick concrete. These containers are sometimes deposited deep underground.

Sometimes radiation can build up in these storage containers and explode them open. This happened on 14 May 1997, at a nuclear waste storage plant in Hanford, Washington State, United States. It could happen in the Chernobyl sarcophagus around reactor four. It could happen in any of thousands of nuclear storage sites all around the world. If it did, it could cause a very serious radiation leak.

ENERGY FACTS

- The average person in Britain uses ten times more energy every year than the average person in India.

- The amount of sunshine that falls on roads in the United States in one year contains twice as much energy as all the coal and oil used worldwide each year.

- The world's largest wind turbines have blades so long that 100 people could stand side by side on them.

- Experts think that underground reserves of oil and coal will run out in about 40 years time.

- A French woman called Marie Curie (1867-1934) was the first scientist to study radiation by working with uranium.

Some people also worry about natural disasters, such as earthquakes or hurricanes, and also terrorist attacks. These could damage nuclear power stations or waste-storage sites and cause radiation leaks too.

Most countries do all they can to make sure nuclear power is produced safely. But accidents can happen. We all need to reduce the amount of electricity we use. We also need to invest money in developing and using safer renewable energy sources.

Wind power is an important form of renewable energy.

TIMELINE

17 Oct 1956   The world's first commercial nuclear power station is opened at Calder Hall, Cumbria, Britain.

10 Oct 1957   A fire breaks out in a reactor at the Windscale nuclear power station in Britain. Radiation leaks over Britain and Europe. An explosion is only narrowly avoided.

3 Jan 1961   The reactor core at a nuclear facility in Idaho, United States, goes out of control. It causes a steam explosion that kills every worker on site.

1960s and 70s   The nuclear industry grows worldwide. In 1963, the US nuclear submarine *Thresher* sinks in the Atlantic Ocean.

Aug 1977   Chernobyl's reactor one goes into operation.

28 Mar 1979   A reactor at the Three Mile Island nuclear power station, Pennsylvania, United States, develops faults in its cooling system. There is a small leak of radiation. There is the danger of an explosion for five days, before the reactor is brought back under control.

May 1979   Chernobyl's reactor two goes into operation.

1980   By now there are 150 nuclear power stations in 21 countries. Most of the stations are in the United States, Britain, the Soviet Union, France, Germany, and Japan.

Jun 1981   Chernobyl's reactor three goes into operation.

Apr 1984   Chernobyl's reactor four goes into operation.

1985	There is a serious accident in Chernobyl's number one reactor. Soviet officials give no details.
26 Apr 1986	Chernobyl's reactor four explodes. A cloud of radiation spreads across Europe to the western United States. Chernobyl's other three reactors are shut down.
3 Oct 1986	Fires and explosions on board Soviet nuclear submarine, *K219*, cause it to sink.
5 Nov 1986	Experts organize the building of a cover, called the sarcophagus, around Chernobyl's reactor four. Chernobyl's reactor two is restarted.
End 1986	Over 800,000 people are involved in the clean-up of Chernobyl and the surrounding area. Chernobyl's reactors one and three are restarted.
Oct 1991	A fire in Chernobyl's reactor two forces station officials to shut it down.
1991	The USSR breaks up into 15 separate countries
Nov 1996	Chernobyl's reactor one is shut down.
Dec 2000	The Chernobyl nuclear power station is shut down completely as the final reactor is switched off.
Apr 2001	Experts start raising funds to rebuild the crumbling sarcophagus around Chernobyl's reactor four.
2005	Work starts on rebuilding the sarcophagus.

GLOSSARY

atom basic tiny building block of matter. Everything is made up of atoms.

cancer serious disease in which some cells in the body start to grow very quickly or in an abnormal way

climate change changes in a region's weather, such as the amount of rain or sunshine it gets

coma when someone is unconscious for a long period of time. They lie as if asleep and do not know what is happening around them.

communism belief that all wealth created by industry and business can be owned by everyone jointly. This wealth should therefore be controlled by the government on behalf of everyone.

convoy cars or buses, etc. travelling together

core centre of a nuclear reactor, where the nuclear reaction happens

DNA tiny, but complicated molecule found in each cell of the body. It carries all the information needed for a normal human being to grow. It also tells what you have inherited from your parents such as your height and the colour of your eyes .

electricity form of energy used to produce light and heat and give power to machinery

engineer person whose job is to design or work with machinery and electrical equipment

evacuate leave an area because of possible danger

exclusion zone area that is cut off and which no one is allowed to enter without special permission

generator piece of machinery which produces electricity

government people who run a country and make sure its laws are applied

graphite type of carbon used to control the speed of a nuclear reaction. The "lead" of your pencil is actually graphite.

hydroelectricity electric power produced from the flowing water from a waterfall or dam driving a turbine

industry factories for making new goods from raw materials, e.g. clothes from cotton

iodine mineral we need to control our bodies' production of energy. Often used to treat thyroid cancer.

nuclear power electricity produced by breaking up the atoms that form uranium

nuclear reactor device in which a nuclear chain reaction is started and controlled, and the resulting heat usually used for power

nuclear weapons weapon of mass destruction whose explosive power comes from a nuclear reaction

nucleus centre of an atom. When the nucleus splits during a nuclear reaction, energy (including heat) and neutrons are released

neutron small part of an atom, found in the nucleus. Neutrons move out of the nucleus at high speed during nuclear reactions. They can then strike other atoms, causing them to release some of their neutrons, and so the reaction continues.

power surge sudden increase in the amount of power being produced

radiation invisible energy particles given off by radioactive materials. It can be harmful to living things.

radioactive material matter such as uranium-235 which is unstable and constantly gives off invisible energy particles

radioactive particles tiny pieces of harmful matter produced by radioactive materials and in nuclear reactions

safety drill exercises and activities practised to make sure that everything will be done safely

scalded burnt by very hot liquid or steam

shutdown when a machine stops because it does not have enough power to carry on working

thyroid cancer cells start to grow uncontrollably in the thyroid, which is in the neck. This can cause breathing problems and the cancer can spread.

toxic poisonous

turbine type of fan that drives other machinery

vote choose someone to do a special job such as to be the prime minister or president

FINDING OUT MORE

BOOKS

20th Century Perspectives: The Russian Revolution, Tony Allan (Heinemann Library, 2002)

Days That Shook the World: The Chernobyl Disaster, Paul Dowswell (Raintree, 2003)

Children in Crisis: Living After Chernobyl: Ira's Story, Linda Walker (World Almanac Library, 2006)

Energy Essentials: Nuclear Energy, Nigel Saunders and Steven Chapman (Raintree, 2005)

Energy Files: Nuclear, Steve Parker (Heinemann Library, 2002)

Witness to History: Hiroshima, Nathanial Harris (Heinemann Library, 2004)

Witness to History: The Collapse of Communism, Stewart Ross (Heinemann Library, 2004)

WEBSITES

www.kiddofspeed.com
Follow the exciting journeys of a young Ukrainian, Elena, as she travels on her motorbike through the ghost towns of the Chernobyl area.

www.chernobyl-international.com
See what the Children of the Chernobyl charity is doing to help young people from the area. You could help, too. Also learn about life there today.

www.aecl.ca./kidszone/atomicenergy
Clear information on the science behind nuclear power. Learn about atoms, molecules, and nuclear fission.

www.nei.org/scienceclub
The young people's pages on the website of the United States' Nuclear Energy Institute shows how nuclear power is generated and how the waste is stored.

www.darvill.clara.net/altenerg
Excellent site about the different types of energy, from nuclear to solar. Written by a teacher.

www.nirs.org
The Nuclear Information and Resource Service is concerned with protecting the planet. Find out more about radioactive waste, radiation, and sustainable energy issues.

FURTHER RESEARCH

If you are interested in finding out more about Chernobyl or nuclear energy, try researching the following topics:

- nuclear power and how it works

- how people live in areas affected by Chernobyl today

- how you can help children affected by Chernobyl

- the bombing of Hiroshima and Nagasaki in Japan in 1945

- President Mikhail Gorbachev and the collapse of the Soviet Union

- alternative energy sources.

INDEX